Globalization

What It Is and How It Works

Globalization

What It Is and How It Works

Lisa A. Crayton and Laura La Bella

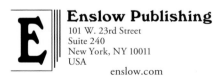

Enslow Publishing
101 W. 23rd Street
Suite 240
New York, NY 10011
USA
enslow.com

Published in 2016 by Enslow Publishing, LLC.
101 W. 23rd Street, Suite 240, New York, NY 10011

Library of Congress Cataloging-in-Publication Data

Crayton, Lisa A., author.
  Globalization : what it is and how it works / Lisa A. Crayton and Laura La Bella.
    pages cm. — (Economics in the 21st century)
  Includes bibliographical references and index.
  Summary: "Describes the concept of globalization and how it affects people's lives today and in the future" — Provided by publisher.
    ISBN 978-0-7660-7244-2
  1. Globalization—Economic aspects—Juvenile literature. 2. Globalization—Juvenile literature.
  I. La Bella, Laura, author. II. Title.
    HF1365.C73 2016
    337—dc23
                    2015032362

Printed in the United States of America

To Our Readers: We have done our best to make sure all website addresses in this book were active and appropriate when we went to press. However, the author and the publisher have no control over and assume no liability for the material available on those websites or on any websites they may link to. Any comments or suggestions can be sent by e-mail to customerservice@enslow.com.

Portions of this text were originally written by Laura La Bella.

Photos Credits: Cover, Rawpixel/Shutterstock.com (left), Anoton Balazh/Shutterstock.com (center), Emi Cristea/Shutterstock.com (right); p. 6 JOKER/Walter G. Allgöwer/ullstein bild via Getty Images; p. 9 © Steven May/Alamy; p. 13 bankerwin/Shutterstock.com; p. 19 Alain Jocard/AFP/Getty Images; p. 20 iStock.com/Paolo Scarlata; p. 22 Jose Cendon/Bloomberg/Getty Images; p. 24 iStock.com/Tito Slack; p. 25 iStock.com/Hocus Focus; p. 27 Bill Pugliano/Getty Images News/Getty Images; p. 29 Hoberman Collection/Universal Images Group/Getty Images; p. 34 iStock.com/Shank Ali; p. 37 Mujahid Safodien/ AFP/Getty Images; p. 38 Spencer Platt/Getty Images North America/Getty Images; p. 40 William87/ Thinkstock; p. 43 iStock.com/Samo Trebizan; p. 45 Zoom Dosso/AFP/Getty Images; p. 48 Kunal Mehta/ Shutterstock.com; p. 50 Skip Bolen/CBS via Getty Images; p. 53 Scott Olson/Getty Images News/ Getty Images; p. 56 Kuznetsandr/Thinkstock; p. 59 Francois Durand/Getty Images Entertainment/ Getty Images; p. 62 Craig Hudson/The Washington Post/Getty Images; p. 64 John Moore/Getty Images News/Getty Images; p. 65 iStock.com/Fire at Dusk; pp. 68, 70 Christopher Gregory/Bloomburg/Getty Images; p. 71 Spencer Platt/Getty Images News/Getty Images; p. 74 Angelos Tzortzinis/AFP/Getty Images; p. 76 Richard James Mendoza/Pacific Press/LightRocket/Getty Images; p. 77 Visions of America/ Universal Images Group/Getty Images.

Contents

In New York City's Chinatown, one can see signs in both Chinese and English. The community caters to Chinese immigrants, but it is still unmistakably an American city.

CHAPTER 1
Many Aspects of Globalization

Walk down a busy street in a city like New York, and it's easy to see how globalization looks in the real world. What has long been called the "melting pot of the world" is home to many cultures. On any given day, it's possible to hear different languages and dialects and smell tantalizing scents of foods from America and other countries. In highly populated tourists areas, like downtown Manhattan, throngs of tourists also converge with their many languages and cultures.

Watching people interact, it is easy to understand how in a flourishing globalization environment, cultures mix and mingle. Exposure to new foods, languages, and cultural activities provides ample opportunities to learn and grow together. As options expand, people can move beyond their own cultures to enjoy what others have to offer. They can sample food they never imagined—like curry oxtails, falafel, arroz con pollo (chicken and rice), even hot dogs! With one bite—or repeated sampling—people may come to love a different flavor, spice, or food texture simply because of globalization.

Schools provide yet another lesson in globalization. Having a new school friend who speaks a different language may spark interest in learning basic phrases to communicate easier. Reading print books and magazines as well as online newspapers and other periodicals provides an additional way to glean the benefit of globalization. Finally, travel opens doors to cultural awareness and understanding when tourists immerse themselves in historical setting. At the same time American tourists experience the awe of the Eiffel Tower in Paris, for example, a French family may be captivated by the Statue of Liberty in Ellis Island, New York.

Globalization has made all of this happen—all over the world.

Local Globalization Scenes

When you visit your local supermarket, you purchase foods from a number of different countries. The grapes you buy might be from Chile. Or, the tomatoes you picked up might have been grown in Mexico.

If you encounter a problem with your computer, you might call a help desk. The person you are talking to might actually live and work in India.

Go to the mall and look at the tags on the clothes that you like to buy. Many will say that the items were made in China, Indonesia, or El Salvador. This is globalization.

Take a look at McDonald's, the largest fast-food restaurant chain in the world, as an example of how a company might approach globalization. McDonald's operates more than thirty-six thousand restaurants in more than one hundred countries around the world. But what is unique about McDonald's is that, throughout the world, its menus reflect the cultures of the countries in which it has restaurants. Here in the United States, stop into any McDonald's and the most popular menu items might be the Big Mac, Chicken McNuggets, and the chain's famous french fries.

In India, however, most people do not eat beef because of their religious beliefs, which include honoring cows as sacred animals. You won't find

The green beans you grab for dinner might come from Egypt.
Fresh crisp veggies are available to you when they're not
in season where you live, thanks to globalization!

hamburgers on the menu at a McDonald's there. Instead, the menu items
at McDonald's restaurants in India are all vegetarian. The most popular
item is the Veggie Burger, which is a hamburger–like sandwich that's made
from potatoes, peas, and carrots and is flavored with Indian spices. Even the
soft–serve ice cream at an Indian McDonald's has a special recipe that does
not use eggs, which is another food item that Hindus in India do not eat.

The same consideration for local tastes and customs is extended to McDonald's restaurants in other countries around the world. In Japan, a Teriyaki McBurger replaces the Big Mac. In Norway, customers can order the McLaks, which is a salmon burger. McDonald's is an example of an American company growing beyond its borders while making sure that local customs are reflected in its menus. This, too, is globalization.

Here to Stay

You can't escape globalization. Globalization—or globalism, as it is also often called—is a term that became popular in the 1980s. It describes the increased international movement of people, knowledge, ideas, products, and money. All of this movement has increased the interconnectedness among the world's populations. It has also made possible the merging of economic, political, social, and cultural identities.

Globalization occurs when companies, products, and services spread to other countries. This starts influencing the cultures and people in those countries. The process of globalization begins when there is a demand for a product that a particular country doesn't have or cannot produce. For example, Americans need gasoline to fuel their cars. Gasoline is produced from oil. But in the United States, there is not enough oil available to meet the demand. Therefore, the United States has to buy oil from other countries in order to create gasoline so that Americans can power their cars and trucks.

While it is a powerful economic force, globalization can be both good and bad. Its effect on the world has been both positive and negative. Globalization can create business opportunities for growing companies. This results in new jobs. It gives people access to products and services that they might not otherwise have in their own countries. And it can aid in a new understanding of cultures, languages, and customs that are different from our own. But globalization has a downside, too. It can cause a loss of native (original or home-gown) culture and heritage as people adapt to outside, foreign influences. It can cause job loss as local businesses build companies in other countries where it costs less to pay workers. Globalization can help some countries grow and expand their workforce, even if it costs other countries much-needed jobs. It can also harm the environment. Globalization is not a new concept. In fact, for thousands of years, countries have bought products from and sold goods to other countries. In the 1800s, the East India Company, which was established in Great Britain, brought cotton, silk, dye, and tea to America's shores for sale. Russia was a major supplier of fur pelts to western Europe and parts of Asia. The pace, scope, and scale of globalization have accelerated dramatically since World War II, especially in the last twenty-five years. Today, there are countless examples of products that are produced in other countries and sold globally. Sometimes, the company that makes the product is based in a different country from that in which the product is actually made. And that product may be sold in a third country or even worldwide.

Many Forms of Globalization

Globalization affects many areas of our society. Among other areas, it has an effect on nations' economic, political, ecological, cultural, and communication systems. A closer look at those five key forms helps us to identify and understand globalization's far-reaching effects on citizens of the world. In turn, it is possible to better comprehend how nations and their cultures affect each other.

Economic Globalization

When we use the words economic globalization, we are really talking about how money travels around the world. Each country has its own businesses, and these businesses often sell their products outside of their own country. When people from many countries around the world are able to buy products that are made and sold by foreign companies—and even work for these companies in some cases—a connection is forged among many different nations. The products we buy and the jobs we have that come from foreign businesses connect us to other countries, their culture, and their peoples.

Economic globalization has been occurring for several thousand years, but it has begun to occur at an increased rate over the last twenty to thirty years. This recent boom has seen the economies of more developed nations partnering with the economies of less developed countries.

For example, Toyota Motor Company is a Japanese carmaker that has manufacturing and assembly factories in more than twenty-five countries, including the United States, Mexico, France, Brazil, Turkey, and Thailand. These factories provide jobs and a paycheck to the workers in these nations. The workers, in turn, spend that money to buy products from not only their own countries but from countries around the world as well. For many companies that make large products like cars, production might occur in more than one country. Cars are often produced in multiple countries by different teams of workers. A new car may be designed in one country, its parts could be manufactured in a second country, and the assembly of those parts might occur in a third country. The breakdown or separating out of jobs is called a division of labor. Today, this division can take place in different countries.

The Toyota Motor Company is based in Japan, but it makes and assembles cars in factories located all over the world: United States, Mexico, France, Brazil, Turkey, and Thailand.

Sometimes, companies in one country produce more goods and services than can be used by its own population. In other words, there aren't enough people in the country to use all of what is made there. The Ivory Coast, located in Africa, is one of the largest producers of cocoa. It sells what it cannot use to other countries that need it. Countries will often pay for goods and services that they either cannot make themselves or are of a higher quality than what they can manufacture. Other times, countries cannot produce enough of a product that is in great need, so they buy products from other countries.

Global Economic Scams

What would you do if a family member e-mailed you or sent you a message through Facebook to say he or she is stuck in a foreign country without cash because of lost personal belongings or because they are the victims of crime? If you're like many people, you will want to respond—and quickly.

Before you do, never send money to anyone without verifying that he or she is indeed someone you know. One quick telephone call, text, or video message to your friend or family member can help you prevent becoming a victim of popular financial scams that take advantage of unsuspecting individuals. Some of these originate out of Africa and India, and they use persuasive tactics that have caused people worldwide to lose millions of dollars. Criminals are almost never caught because it is impossible to track their actual locations. Be smart: don't fall for such scams. And, if you receive any communications like this, report it to your e-mail or social media provider. This may help block scammers from cheating other people, too.

This is the case with the earlier example of oil. The United States uses more than 25 percent of the world's oil, but it produces only 3 percent of the world's oil supply. To keep cars running and homes heated, the United States must purchase oil from other countries in order to fill the demand.

Economic globalization is one of the few types of globalization that can be measured. We can look at four different categories to see if economic globalization has increased or decreased around the world. These four categories are as follows:

- Goods and services, which are measured in terms of the number of products that are exported (sold and sent to other countries from the United States) or imported (sold and sent to the United States from other countries)

- Migration, or movement of people, which allows us to watch how many people come into a country to find work or how many are forced to leave to find work outside that country

- Capital, or money, which helps gauge how much each nation makes as a result of products and people flowing back and forth

- Technology, which tells us how inventions and innovations in communication, computers, and manufacturing influence globalization

Political Globalization

Political globalization is how governments from different countries get along with one another. The United States has countries that it is very friendly with (such as England, France, Japan, and Canada) and other countries that it is not so friendly with (Iran, North Korea, Cuba, and Syria, for example).

Technology, such as the Internet, cell phones, jet planes, and satellite television, has connected people in different countries, whether they be friend or foe. This connectivity has increased our awareness of one another because we can see and talk to each other instantly. This allows us to see what other countries are doing and encourages our governments to develop relationships with one other, even if there are disagreements, suspicion, or bad feelings. Those relationships can be helpful when we form partnerships to help defend ourselves against common enemies, to deliver help following a natural disaster (such as a hurricane or earthquake), and to exchange scientific information like cures for diseases.

Ecological Globalization

Ecological globalization refers to the influence people and companies have on the world's ecosystems. An ecosystem consists of all the plants, animals, and microorganisms that work together in the environment of a specific area. A rain forest is an example of an ecosystem. Ecosystems are constantly changing. The movement of air over the surface of the earth, the flow of water in rivers, and the migration of animals and people across a landscape all cause changes in ecosystems.

For example, the West Coast of the United States is affected by the air pollution that is created in China and other Asian countries. Tiny airborne particles of pollution are drifting over the Pacific Ocean from coal-fired power plants, smelters, dust storms, and diesel trucks in Asia. This causes harm to the air and water quality and to the general environmental health of American cities on the West Coast, such as San Francisco.

To help keep the environment healthy on a global scale, people and companies worldwide must take into consideration the effects that their activities have on communities in countries outside of their own.

Cultural Globalization

Cultural globalization refers to the sharing of ideas and cultural products. The United States is the largest exporter of movies and, thus, is a large exporter of American culture. Other countries produce films, too. In fact, India produces more films a year than Hollywood does, and Japan and Hong Kong are leaders in movie production as well. However, many of these films are not seen outside of their home countries. Indian films are produced mostly for Indian audiences, and films from Japan and Hong Kong are shown outside of Asia in small "art house" movie theaters. Foreign films often have trouble getting distributed and shown in the United States, and they often don't come out on DVD.

Hollywood movies may showcase American ways of life, but the film industry is not uniquely American. Hollywood is known for finding the best actors, actresses, and directors from around the world and making them stars. *Pirates of the Caribbean* star Orlando Bloom is from England, *Chicago*'s Catherine Zeta-Jones is from Wales, *Star Wars*' Ewan McGregor is from Scotland, and *X-Men*'s Hugh Jackman is from Australia. Even some of Hollywood's top directors are from outside America. Ridley Scott, director of *Gladiator, Kingdom of Heaven*, and *Blade Runner*, is from England. Peter Jackson, the director of the three *Lord of the Rings* films, is from New Zealand. The *Harry Potter* movies, which have become the biggest film series in movie history, are based on books by an English author—J. K. Rowling—and feature a largely English cast. Some of Hollywood's biggest studios are also foreign-owned. Japan's Sony Company owns Columbia Pictures, and Vivendi Universal is French-owned.

A cultural phenomenon that has caught on in the United States is manga. *Manga* in Japanese basically means "comics," and it has become a large part of Japan's publishing industry. Manga stories include a broad range of subjects, from action-adventure, romance, and sports to historical drama, comedy,

Caring Around the Globe: Asian Tsunami Relief Aid

On December 26, 2004, an earthquake in the Indian Ocean caused a tsunami, a series of massive waves that can cause immense flooding and destruction. Particularly hard-hit were India, Indonesia, Sri Lanka, and Thailand. More than 225,000 people were killed, tens of thousands were injured, and ten million found themselves homeless. The world's response to this tragedy is an example of political globalization. Governments and companies from around the world provided help to the countries affected by the natural disaster. More than fifty-five countries offered military help and monetary aid. In addition, millions of people donated money to help, and companies worldwide offered their support. Pharmaceutical (drug) companies like Pfizer, Johnson & Johnson, and Bristol-Myers Squibb provided medical supplies and drugs. Beverage companies, such as Iceland Spring Water, supplied fresh water. And humanitarian organizations—including the International Red Cross, Catholic Relief Services, Oxfam, the United Nations, and World Jewish Aid—donated medical supplies and services, sent volunteers, or raised money to help the tsunami victims rebuild their homes and communities.

When a natural disaster hits in any part of the world, people from countries across the globe pitch in to send supplies and people to help with the recovery.

The film adaptations of the Harry Potter books were wildly popular in the United States and all over the world, with the author and much of the cast from England.

science fiction, and horror. *Pokémon* is probably the most popular example of Japanese manga in the United States. The vast majority of manga sold in America is written, drawn, inked, and published in Japan. However, a small but growing American manga industry has sprung up in recent years.

Globalization of Communication

Globalization of communication is how the world's people talk to one another through more advanced technology. One hundred years ago, people communicated with each other by sending a letter or a telegram. Over the course of the last century, we have developed new ways to reach out to people instantaneously, even if they are in countries on the other side of the world. Today, cell phones, e-mail, text messaging, webcams, and the Internet allow us to express our ideas instantly with others. Telecommunications companies like Verizon, Sprint, and AT&T all compete against each other to provide the fastest and easiest ways to communicate with other people via landline phone, cell phone, e-mail, and the Internet.

These technologies allow for a greater amount of information to be exchanged back and forth between people and places that traditionally have not communicated with one another. As a result, there has been an increase in cross-cultural communication, understanding, and curiosity. Anyone with an Internet connection can access foreign news outlets—like the *Central Daily News* in North Korea, the *New Zealand Herald* in New Zealand, or the *People's Daily Newspaper* in China—just as easily as he or she can access CNN or *USA Today*.

A Nike store in Bogotá, Colombia, illustrates how globalization allows major corporations to find success beyond their native countries.

CHAPTER 2

Globalization: Its Causes and Effects

Sell hamburgers, fries, and beverages to busy people who want to eat quickly, don't have time to make home-cooked meals, or want to dine out cheaply. Manufacture footwear that is not only fashionable but also useful for wearing during sports or other physical activity. With a single, successful business idea like these, companies can grow from humble beginnings into major corporations. As many do, they often look to expand their customer base and thereby increase potential profits. That is a key reason many familiar corporations, such as McDonald's and Nike, expand into other countries. This globalization strategy works so well that successful international companies often boast income or work-forces far exceeding that of small countries! How do businesses grow so big and expand internationally? The answer is globalization.

Globalization occurs for many reasons. There have been advances in transportation and technology that make it much easier to produce goods and move them around the world quickly and relatively inexpensively. The creation and development of information and communications technology, particularly the Internet, allow people to raise their awareness of different cultures and places. People are now much more knowledgeable about foreign foods and cultures, different languages, and international problems than they were in the past. It is now easier for people to communicate with others in faraway places and even connect to one another through the Internet or satellite communications. Advances in communication technology help to spread globalization. Communication among people is now easier, faster, and cheaper (or even free in some cases) with the Internet and e-mail. The media, too, can now reach worldwide audiences, instantly broadcasting news and entertainment worldwide.

Cost cutting is another important reason for globalization. Many well-known companies have a global presence and conduct business in countries around the world. They often open factories in other nations for a variety

Businesses like Burger King are popular everywhere that people need a fast, inexpensive meal, so they are able to expand their customer base into many countries.

Technology is often right at our fingertips, making it easier than ever to order goods from another country, learn about other cultures, and communicate with people almost anywhere!

of economic reasons. Labor may be less expensive in other countries, which can save companies money. International trade also makes it easier to manufacture goods in the countries that consume them, cutting down on shipping costs.

Globalization is a complex issue. There are many people who are supportive of globalization. They believe it is a way to help poorer countries develop their economies and improve the lives of their citizens. But there are also those who are against globalization and think it ultimately hurts the workers and economies of both the home country and its foreign trading partners.

Thumbs Up for Globalization

Those who support globalization say that it has led to an increase in communication between peoples. It has had a positive impact on our environment. It has helped spread technology around the world. And it has aided in the movement of people who choose to live and work in other countries.

Supporters of globalization say that it can increase economic success and offer opportunities for developing nations, too. These opportunities can be an increase in the jobs available and higher pay for workers. Globalization can also lead to enhanced freedoms for the people living in developing countries. For example, workers might organize a union that will represent them in order to gain pay increases and better benefits, such as health care. Proponents also say that globalization can lead to the more efficient allocation (providing and spreading) of resources.

Globalization can result in competition between international companies. This keeps businesses sharp and forces them to develop new products and improve existing ones. Consumers benefit from this competition because it means that they have greater choices, a broader range of quality in the items offered, and, often, lower prices.

The spread of technology has been a positive outcome of globalization. Companies are establishing factories and offices in different countries, bringing with them new technologies that might not reach some underdeveloped countries otherwise.

Globalization also means the spread of people. Because globalization has increased the flow of information, improved communication, made transportation faster and cheaper, and increased the number of jobs available in some countries, it has caused workers to move or migrate to other countries.

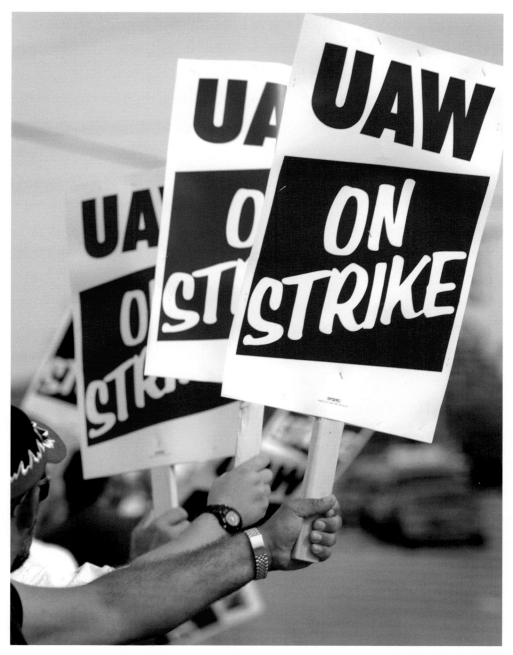

Globalization supporters argue that it can mean more freedom for
people in developing countries. They can organize a union to fight
for higher pay and better working conditions, for example.

The migration of people is not new. For centuries, people have left their homes in search of better opportunities, both in and outside of their own countries. Globalization has just added a new dimension. As businesses expand to include operations in foreign countries, migration becomes a necessity for many.

Globalization has helped to improve living conditions in lesser-developed countries. Many people who didn't have access to basic necessities now have better food choices, basic shelter, and decent clothing and live longer and healthier lives because of globalization. Some of the world's fastest economic growth and development are occurring in some of the poorest countries, such as India, China, and Indonesia.

Opposition to Globalization

The term anti-globalization is used to describe the opinion of people and groups that oppose globalization. Some countries may adopt anti-globalization stances, making it harder for people, goods, and culture to spread to and from those countries. Those who are anti-globalization believe that globalization can have a negative impact on employment, culture, and the environment.

Globalization has given companies the opportunity to establish themselves in other nations. Some companies have used this as a way to save money and pay workers in developing countries less than they would pay workers in the developed countries where they are based. Some countries do not have strong health, labor, and safety laws, which are in place to protect workers from harmful chemicals, limit the number of hours a company can require of workers, and guard workers from workplace hazards. Many companies have moved their manufacturing operations to countries where these laws do not exist.

Without these protections, companies are able to make their employees work long hours for unfair pay and put their health at risk by making them work in unsafe conditions. The abundance of cheap labor in poorer, developing nations is giving rich, developed ones no reason to solve the problem of economic inequality between nations. While these workers are free to leave their jobs, they may not have another job to go to. That means they will not have an income and will not have a way to make money to support themselves or their families.

Opponents to globalization point out that not all countries pay their workers a fair wage, force people to work long hours, and don't maintain a safe working environment.

Safety First!

Many companies open factories in countries like China and India because of cheaper labor costs, less restrictive safety requirements, or other factor that makes doing business cheaper abroad than in a native locale. Sometimes, however, the factory conditions may hinder rather than benefit business. In recent years, for example, factory fires have caused millions of dollars in property damage and hundreds of deaths. For example, in 2013, five garment factories shared a building in Bangladesh, India. When the building collapsed, more than one thousand employees of those factories were killed. The extensive loss of life prompted calls for better, more effective safety standards. Safety is an area of globalization that will likely attract continued scrutiny as world leaders continually hold companies accountable for safer workplaces.

Another result of jobs being sent overseas is increased competition between workers. Millions of American workers are now facing more competition from workers in less developed countries who are willing to work for far lower wages. In 2004, the AFL-CIO (a leading labor union) reported that an estimated 406,000 US jobs were sent overseas, compared to 204,000 jobs in 2001. More recently, according to the Economic Policy Institute, "Growth in the U.S. goods trade deficit with China between 2001 and 2013 eliminated or displaced 3.2 million U.S. jobs, 2.4 million (three-fourths) of which were in manufacturing. These lost manufacturing jobs account for about two-thirds of all U.S. manufacturing jobs lost or displaced between December, 2001 and December 2013."

Is Anything Really "Made in America" Anymore?

There was once a popular bumper sticker that appeared on the back of American-made cars that read, "Real Americans Buy American." But are products really made in America anymore? American automobiles are a great example of American products that are not made entirely in the United States. Chevrolet, a popular US car and truck company, builds many of its vehicles in Mexico with parts imported from other countries. The Ford Motor Company has plants all around the world. Its plant in Germany employs many workers who have emigrated from Turkey.

An American car designer created the Toyota Camry. Toyota, a Japanese automaker, owns a plant in Newport Beach, California, where the company has a design center. Its Camry was designed in California and built in a Toyota plant in Kentucky from mostly American parts. The car is test-driven on a track in Arizona. So, it's possible that not one piece of the Toyota your parents own was made outside the United States, even though it is a foreign car. This same idea can be applied to so many products, from cars and trucks to television sets, furniture, and clothing.

A loss of cultural identity can occur when two or more cultures collide. There is a risk that each country could lose some of the aspects of its heritage that make it unique. There is also a risk for Westernization, which is the process in which non-Western societies adopt Western culture. "Western culture" refers to the cultures of European countries and the United States. It is a combination of industry, technology, law, politics, economics, lifestyle, diet, language, religion, and values. Some underdeveloped countries may become more modern or less traditional due to the influence of Western ideals, resulting in dramatic changes to their age-old culture.

While globalization can help inspire the solving of our environmental problems, it can also add to these problems. In the same way that health, labor, and safety laws can differ from country to country, so, too, can environmental regulations. For example, some countries allow businesses to be less concerned with the pollution generated from manufacturing and do not limit the amount of pollution that a company generates, causing widespread environmental dangers.

More Pros Than Cons?

The positives of globalization often seem to outweigh the negatives. It can increase the wealth of poorer countries. It creates employment. It can result in global problem solving through shared approaches to pressing issues like protecting the environment or curing deadly diseases. It brings nations together to help one another in times of crisis. Globalization has the potential to make our world a better, more cooperative and peaceful place to live in.

Ten Great Questions to Ask a Financial Adviser

1 Should I invest in foreign companies?

2 Are there risks to investing in companies that have a global presence?

3 Can any financial adviser manage stocks and investments in global companies?

4 What are offshore investments?

5 What is diversification?

6 What happens to my overseas investments if there is a war or other international crisis?

7 Is there an international regulatory agency monitoring and overseeing global markets like the SEC does for the US economy?

8 Does my financial adviser need additional certifications or licenses to give me advice?

9 Do I pay American taxes on my foreign investments? Would I pay foreign taxes on them?

10 How are foreign investments different from US-based investments?

Many of the video games you like to play after school are completely created in foreign countries. Globalization allows us access to products from almost any place in the world.

CHAPTER 3
Windows to the World

Our world is more diverse and interesting because of globalization. It has expanded available choices in clothing, food, cars, entertainment, and other everyday essential and non-essential items. Furthermore, it has provided a means of learning new languages and experiencing different cultures without the need to actually visit or move abroad. These are some of the exciting ways in which globalization's effects are felt in America and nations around the world.

Think about all the items you own, from your clothes and toys to your books, movies, board games, and video games. Many of these products were created, designed, manufactured, or developed in foreign countries. Globalization has opened up a worldwide market for companies. Today, people have access to many products from different countries. When you go shopping, you now have access to a lot more goods.

Globalization's effects reach farther than consumption, however, to include working together as a global community to solve a range of problems, from diseases and illnesses to environmental concerns. As we've seen so far, globalization has in many ways drawn the world closer. As a global community, we share responsibility for the effects globalization has on the world.

Environmental Effects

Globalization has drawn attention to the environment, which affects all of us. Global warming and other environmental concerns, such as melting glaciers and ice caps, air pollution, dwindling supplies of freshwater, and the dramatic changes in our climate, affect every human being on the planet. Because of this, there has been an increase in the number of worldwide environmental organizations that are working together to help coordinate international environmental policies.

The United Nations Environment Programme helps developing countries put into practice environmentally sound policies. It was created in June 1972, following the United Nations Conference on the Human Environment. Although the organization is headquartered in Nairobi, Kenya, it has six regional offices covering the geographic areas of Africa, Asia and the Pacific, Europe, Latin America and the Caribbean, North America, and western Asia. According to its website, the United Nations Environment Programme's mission is to "provide leadership and encourage partnership in caring for the environment by inspiring, informing, and enabling nations and peoples to improve their quality of life without compromising that of future generations."

Greenpeace is one of the world's most effective and attention-getting environmental activist groups. It is dedicated to the protection and conservation of the environment and the promotion of peace throughout the world. The organization has worked hard to make a number of positive environmental changes around the globe. It was successful in persuading major computer and electronics makers like Dell, Hewlett-Packard, Apple, and Sony Ericsson to eliminate the use of toxic chemicals in the manufacture of their products. Greenpeace also takes on land developers that are more

Greenpeace workers, like these demonstrators in South Africa, tirelessly bring attention to environmental issues and concerns all over the world.

interested in making money by building in natural areas than in protecting delicate and endangered ecosystems. For example, it secured a rare victory in preserving a large area of the Amazon rain forest from being destroyed by loggers. Greenpeace has a worldwide presence, with national and regional offices in more than forty countries.

Communication Effects

Communication is an important element of globalization. Thanks to globalization, there has been an increase in information flowing between countries. People around the world are more connected to each other than ever before. Both the Internet and satellite television have made it possible to read newspapers, watch news broadcasts, and see movies and shows originating in foreign countries. As societies and economies embrace new communication technologies, the peoples of the world become a closer-knit community, despite the great physical and cultural distances between us.

Let's look back at a historical event that shows how news can affect the world and connect us all. The day is September 11, 2001. You live and work in New York City, but today you are in Paris, France, on a business trip. It is early afternoon, Paris time, and you take a break from your meetings to go back to your hotel room. You turn on the television and flip through

When the devastation of September 11, 2001, occurred, people were able to get information about what was going on almost immediately, via television, radio, and the Internet.

the channels. Suddenly, on one of the twenty-four-hour cable news stations, you see an image of the twin towers of the World Trade Center in New York City on fire. You sit and watch history unfold, live and unedited on the television set. You might be alone in your hotel room in Paris, but at the same time you are connected to millions of others who are watching the very same images at the very same moment from locations all around the world. You are all sharing the same experience at the same time.

Now, imagine what it must have been like on December 7, 1941, when Japanese forces attacked Pearl Harbor in Hawaii. The Internet did not exist in the 1940s and neither did CNN. Television, for that matter, was in its infancy, with commercial television stations just beginning to get broadcasting licenses from the government. It took hours for news of the surprise attack to reach most Americans, mostly through their radios. It took more than an entire day before the full story, along with photographs of burning and sinking battleships, made it into newspaper articles and television news reports. Gradually, word spread farther and farther until the whole world knew of the tragedy, several days after the attack on Pearl Harbor.

Globalization has made it possible for magazines, newspapers, and other news outlets to share information on global events quickly and accurately. CNN, founded in 1980, is one of the world's leading news agencies. It has international divisions that deliver the news in Spanish, Turkish, Korean, and Japanese.

Major news publications, such as *Time* magazine, have international editions. *Time*, first published in the United States, now has a European edition called *Time Europe*, which is published in London, England. *Time Europe* covers Europe, the Middle East, Africa, and Latin America. An

Asian edition, *Time Asia*, is based in Hong Kong. The South Pacific edition, covering Australia, New Zealand, and the Pacific Islands, is based in Sydney, Australia. Both global reporting and international offices increase our understanding of those who live in different parts of the world.

Cultural Effects

Globalization can expose people to new ideas and experiences. These ideas are often adopted, and the values and traditions of a culture can change and evolve. As a result, if the change is extreme or sudden enough, it may result in a loss of cultural identity.

Food is an area in which this occurs most commonly. In many countries, food is an integral part of culture. But with globalization, outside influences

When Starbucks CEO Howard Schultz saw how Italians lingered over and savored their coffee, he was inspired to change Americans' approach to the hot drink. Globalization exposed him to new ideas.

can change the role that food plays in a culture. Take, for example, Starbucks, the American coffee company. Originally, Starbucks was a company that sold coffee beans. It did not sell brewed coffee in its stores. This all changed when Howard Schultz, the company's chief executive officer (CEO), traveled to Italy and observed the importance of coffee to the Italians.

Coffee in Italy is more than a drink. It is part of the Italian way of life. Italians sit in cafes and leisurely savor a cup of coffee. In the United States,

Lifelong Lessons

Can fourth graders solve world problems like global warming, constant war, cultural conflict, and poverty? Perhaps not in the real world—yet. But, a game developed by an educator from Virginia has allowed them to do so in an engaging, learning environment for several decades.

John Hunter created the "World Peace Game" as a teaching tool to help students better understand global concerns and comprise possible solutions to fifty questions challenging the world. Students assume influential decision-making roles and must work together to see satisfactory solutions that benefit multiple countries. The game is won when each of those questions is answered. Over the years, the game has developed into an interactive, multi-level game that continues to stimulate student interest in world affairs while sparking their collective solutions. For more information about the game, visit http://www.worldpeacegame.org.

however, it is common for people to buy a cup of coffee and take it with them to the office or to drink in the car while driving to work. Schultz saw an opportunity to change the way that Americans drink coffee. He made Starbucks cafes places to sit, relax, and sample different brews of coffee while casually meeting with friends or working on a laptop.

Energy Effects

Globalization has led to an increase in energy use worldwide. There are many different types of energy. There are fossil fuels, which are formed in the earth from plant or animal remains. Oil is one of the most popular fossil fuels. Nuclear power is energy that is generated through nuclear fission, which occurs when one atom splits into two. There are also renewable and alternative energy sources. These sources include biofuels, ethanol, wind power, hydrogen power and fuel cells, solar power, and hydropower. Renewable energy is using existing flows of energy, as well as natural processes, to generate energy for use. Supplies cannot be depleted or used up. Instead, they renew or replenish themselves or are constantly available.

Water is a great example of a renewable energy source. Hydropower plants can create energy from the flow of water. The amount of available energy in moving water is determined by how fast or slow it flows through a riverbed or over a waterfall. The water flows through pipes called penstocks. As it flows through penstocks, it turns large turbines, which cause generators to produce electricity. This electricity is carried to users by power lines.

There is more energy usage today worldwide than ever before. Since 1980, the amount has increased by 57 percent globally. The United States has seen an increase of 28 percent. This amount of energy usage is equivalent to having twenty-two lightbulbs burning nonstop for every person on the planet.

Two countries whose energy usage has increased the most are India and China. Both countries are quickly developing more businesses and building more manufacturing plants. India and China also have huge populations. The more people that live in a country, the more energy that country uses.

Globalization has allowed these now developing countries to make great advances in terms of technology and prosperity. With these advances come more energy-consuming tools, machines, cars, and appliances, just like those the Western world has enjoyed for decades. The result, however positive to these nations' citizens, is an enormous and growing strain on the earth's resources and ecological health.

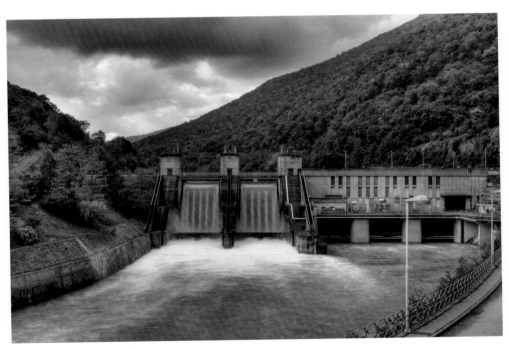

With increased globalization comes increased energy use. Renewable energy sources, like a hydropower plant that can harness the energy of water, are more important than ever.

Health Effects

Globalization is promoting the rapid spread and effective treatment of highly contagious diseases. It isn't difficult to imagine how increases in international commerce and the movement of people might influence health. More products are made and sold in more places around the world than ever before. People now travel farther and to more exotic locations, placing them in contact with other people in areas where specific diseases are found. This greater movement of goods and people increases the chance for the spread of certain diseases around the world. Just like products, diseases can travel across oceans and national borders. So, diseases like AIDS, malaria, and tuberculosis can infect more people. Mosquitoes that carry malaria have been found aboard planes thousands of miles from their primary habitats. The outbreak of mad cow disease in several European countries is another example of how trade can promote the spread of dangerous diseases.

Mad cow disease was first discovered in 1986 in cattle raised in Great Britain. The disease is an incurable, fatal brain disease that affects the nervous system of a cow. It causes the animal to act strangely and lose control of its ability to do normal things, such as walk. It is believed that people who ingest poorly cooked beef from an infected cow can contract the deadly human version of this disease.

In 2007 and 2008, tainted Chinese milk products and pet food created a worldwide health scare. These are examples of how trade can promote the spread of dangerous diseases and negatively affect the safety of the food supply.

Globalization can provide the solution as well as the problem, however. It can improve access to medicines, medical information, and training that

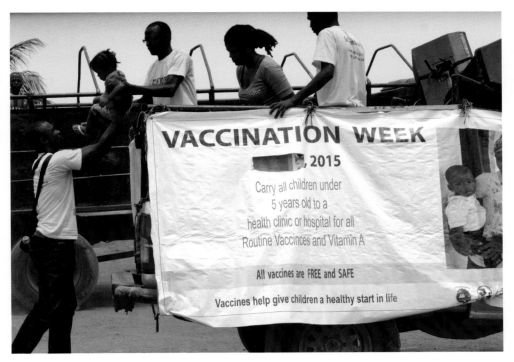

Globalization also exposes people to new germs and diseases,
which their bodies may not be able to fight off. Vaccines
and medicines have to be more readily available.

can help treat or cure diseases. Drug companies and governments now have
the ability to ship drugs to remote parts of the world affected by epidem-
ics, providing medical care to areas that they might not have been able to
reach before.

Impact on Poor Countries

Through globalization, poorer countries can raise their standards of living
by trading and partnering with rich countries in order to create economic
growth. The money made through trading and inviting foreign companies

The "McDonaldization" of the World

American companies can have a strong influence on the customs of other countries. McDonald's is one company that has had a profound effect on children's behavior in China. In the past, it was not considered proper for Chinese children to buy food with their own money. Instead, they were expected to eat the food that their parents chose for them. With its fun-loving clown mascot and kid-friendly Happy Meals, McDonald's markets heavily to children. Because of this, Chinese children began to show an interest in choosing their own food when going to McDonald's. After some time, it became a more common practice for Chinese children to select and buy food with their own money.

McDonald's also popularized birthday parties in China. Festivities marking a child's birth date were not often held in China. McDonald's helped influence this new tradition by successfully promoting American-style birthday parties as part of its marketing strategy. This shows that the spread of American companies in foreign countries can have unexpected cultural consequences.

in to set up shop allows governments to provide better health care, education, and safety to their people. This is called development.

According to the World Bank, which is a vital source of financial and technical assistance to developing countries, poverty worldwide has decreased because of globalization. It reported that in 2011, 17 percent of people in the developing world were living at or below $1.25 a day. That was significantly less than 43 percent in 1990 and 52 percent in 1981. That equated to just over one billion people living on less than $1.25 a day in 2011, compared with 1.91 billion in 1990 and 1.93 billion in 1981. Globalization is creating opportunities for poor countries to partner with rich countries, giving poor countries greater access to wealth over time. When a company builds a manufacturing plant in a developing country, that country's citizens have access to jobs. Sometimes, these jobs come with training so that workers know how to use the necessary equipment. This is a form of education. The money the workers take home with them allows them to buy better food, clothes, and housing for their families. Perhaps they can even save for a formal education for their kids, who will then go on to more comfortable lives with more opportunities than their parents had.

As the economy in these poor countries grows, the nations, their citizens, and their infrastructure (roads, bridges, tunnels, railways, airports, sewers, wells, etc.) become more developed. Globalization has had a big and positive impact on many of these nations.

You can see globalization in action right in your neighborhood grocery store. Foods and products from all kinds of cultures from around the world are more readily available all the time.

CHAPTER 4
Bridging Cultures

Walk into the any major shopping mall and you'll quickly see globalization in action. In clothing stores, apparel made in the United States, China, and India is available for children and adults. In footwear venues, Adidas (Germany), Reebok (Great Britain), and Fila (Italy) are available to buy, along with those from American companies. At a sporting goods store, it's possible to buy yoga, basketball, or volleyball equipment—each popular in different countries across the world. Feeling hungry? Head on over to the food court where hot dogs and hamburgers may be sold, as well international fare from Italy (pizza), India (curry chicken), China (vegetable lo mein), or Greece (gyros).

The ability to purchase these things without leaving American soil is amazing! Indeed, the mall is an ideal point of reference showing how globalization enables Americans to explore and experience different cultures. From it, it's apparent that globalization expands choices, enabling us to sample different aspects of other cultures and include them in our everyday life. We see the benefit of having global apparel, products, entertainment, food, and other items and how those contribute to making our lives richer and more satisfying.

Understanding "Americanization"

As globalization spreads and many American companies expand into foreign countries, the idea of Americanization has emerged as a concern. Americanization is a term that describes the dominating and transformative influence the United States has on the cultures of other countries. American television, film, and music are considered to be the biggest agents of Americanization in other countries. American TV shows are broadcast around the world. At the Monte Carlo TV Awards in 2014, *Modern Family* was among the most watched show internationally.

The most popular drama television series around the world was *NCIS: Naval Criminal Investigative Service.* Yet, just as Americanization influences

When popular American shows like *NCIS* are broadcast all over the world, they may give people in other countries an incorrect impression of life and people in the United States.

other countries, other countries influence the culture of the United States. This is not a new phenomenon. The United States has long absorbed influences from around the world, beginning with those of its former colonial masters: France, Spain, the Netherlands, and Great Britain. Its long history of immigration has expanded the range of influences dramatically. In fact, the United States is a nation of immigrants. It is defined by the immigrant experience. As such, it provides a great example of how cultures come into contact and communicate with each other, trade influences, and ultimately create something original and powerful—a new culture with its own evolving traditions.

Many American products are not as all-American as they may seem. Levi Strauss, the creator of blue jeans, was a German immigrant who came to America and settled in San Francisco, California. He created jeans by combining denim cloth, which was originally woven in a French town, with genes, a style of pants worn by sailors from Genoa, Italy. So, Levi's jeans are, in fact, an American twist on French fabric and Italian style. There are many similar examples of distinct cultures spreading, mixing, and becoming popular in different parts of the world, far from their origins.

Sports often spread across the globe and become fixtures in their new homelands. Many of the world's most popular sports, most notably soccer, came by way of Britain or Latin America. Both football and baseball have at least some of their origins in England. Asian martial arts like judo, karate, and kickboxing are now widely practiced by people of all ages worldwide. Yoga, which originated in India, has also swept the world.

Food is another area in which tastes have changed. In the United States, there are hundreds of fast-food restaurant chains like McDonald's, Burger King, and Wendy's. But in England, the favorite takeout food is Indian. In fact, Indian restaurants outnumber McDonald's six to one in England. And despite the hamburger's central importance to Americans, pizza is actually far more popular worldwide.

Fashion is another influential cultural force that has spread from country to country. Some of the biggest fashion houses and designers in the world are from Europe. Gucci, Armani, and Versace are all Italian designers. Chanel and Hermès are French. Sweden's Hennes & Mauritz (known as H&M in America) and Spain's Zara compete against the American stores Gap and Old Navy. American sneaker companies like Nike and New Balance compete, as noted previously, against international companies, such as Adidas, Reebok, and Fila. American exports are often tailored to local tastes. MTV Asia promotes pop stars from Thailand and plays rock music sung in Mandarin, a Chinese dialect. MTV Europe features European singers and bands, and it even hosts a European version of the MTV Video Music Awards. CNN en Español offers a Latin American view on world news.

Global Soft Drink Giant

The Coca-Cola Company is the world's largest beverage company and one of the biggest corporations in the United States. It is best known for Coca-Cola, a soft drink invented by John Stith Pemberton in 1886. The company now makes more than four hundred different beverages. These include Diet Coke, Cherry Coke, Vanilla Coke, Sprite, Minute Maid juices, and Powerade sports drinks. The company's biggest seller, however, has always remained Coca-Cola.

The company has a huge global presence. Coca-Cola operates in more than two hundred nations and has more than three hundred bottling partners

Coca-Cola is the biggest seller of all the Coca-Cola Company's products. The company makes the beverage all over the world, which provides the jobs that help local economies.

worldwide. Every two days, one billion Coca-Colas are sold. The company spends $1 billion annually on advertising and marketing worldwide to make sure that its products remain highly visible and attractive.

In all countries where it is bottled, Coca-Cola helps grow the local economy. Coca-Cola does this by selling its soft drink as a concentrate to bottlers, who then add water, sugar, and carbon dioxide according to a specific formula provided by the company. These bottlers are responsible for selling the product. To sell Coke, they need to buy cases, bottles, coolers, uniforms for workers, and various other items. The Coca-Cola Company encourages its bottlers to make deals with local companies to provide these materials. By doing this, Coca-Cola bottlers spend money in their own communities, spurring the local economy and generating goodwill.

How popular is Coca-Cola around the globe? Aside from being one of the most important worldwide sponsors of the Olympic Games, it is also one of the most heavily consumed beverages on the planet. According to the company's website, if all the Coca-Cola ever produced was contained in eight-ounce bottles and laid end to end, they would reach to the moon and back 1,677 times. Coca-Cola has been the number-one soft drink in France since 1966. Belgium is ranked among the world's top twenty consumers of Coca-Cola products. In Italy, consumers drink an average of one hundred servings of Coca-Cola products per person each year.

Share One With?

What's in a name? Everything, if you ask the many consumers flocking to stores to find twenty-ounce bottles of Coca-Cola, Diet Coke, and Coke Zero with their names on it. In 2010, Coca-Cola introduced and began selling those sized beverages with labels bearing one of 250 most popular first names among American teens and Millennials, people younger than age thirty-five. It launched the successful promotional campaign in Australia and has since introduced them in more than fifty countries. The buzz has been high on social media, particularly, with consumers snapping photos of themselves drinking the beverage with a label sporting their name or that of friends or family members.

McDonald's: World Leader in Globalization

McDonald's began in 1940 when two brothers, Dick and Mac McDonald, opened a restaurant in San Bernardino, California. The company that is now known as McDonald's, however, really took off in 1955. That is when Ray Kroc franchised the restaurant. In the McDonald's franchising system, an owner purchases the right to operate a restaurant under the McDonald's name and must offer standard McDonald's products and service. The owner must also follow all of the corporate rules for operating the restaurant. Kroc later purchased the McDonald brothers' restaurants and was the man who led the growth of McDonald's from just a few scattered hamburger stands to a massive fast-food chain with a global presence.

As McDonald's expanded into international locations, the company became a symbol of globalization and the American way of life. McDonald's now operates more than thirty-one thousand restaurants in 107 countries. It serves fifty-two million people daily. Before the introduction of McDonald's overseas, the idea of standardized fast-food restaurants elsewhere in the world was almost unknown. McDonald's became the first company to export America's love of fast food, even though not all McDonald's restaurants serve the exact same menu. In fact, McDonald's creates regional menus to conform to local tastes and customs. In Egypt, for example, you can order a McFalafel. In Japan, a burger made of seaweed is a top seller. In Taiwan, kids' meals are served in reusable metal containers in keeping with local custom.

The company has also let popular local products influence its menus and product offerings. For instance, McDonald's in Australia was the first to serve specialty coffees. Fancy types of breads in France and Italy became

Although McDonald's features American fast food, it does offer locally popular products on its menus around the world, such as at this restaurant in Vologda, Russia.

sandwich rolls in those countries. In fact, if you take a look at the official websites of McDonald's franchises around the world, you will find that nearly all of them are locally owned. Most buy at least half their supplies from local growers. This has a positive effect on the local economy, area farmers, and prices. (The farther food travels before being consumed, the more it will cost.) McDonald's understands that buying from local farmers and producers not only cuts down on shipping costs but also creates wealth in those communities.

McDonald's has helped to change cultures, too. In the book *Golden Arches East*, by James L. Watson, McDonald's restaurants are credited with introducing the concept of forming orderly lines to wait in before ordering, as opposed to rushing the counter, as was the tradition in Korea. In Hong Kong, public bathrooms were notoriously dirty and unsanitary. McDonald's clean, sterile facilities forced competing restaurants in the city to literally clean up their acts.

The Disney Factor

The Walt Disney Company is a massive global corporation. It is one of the largest media, entertainment, and merchandising enterprises in the world. Brothers Walt and Roy Disney founded it in 1923. Originally, it was an animation studio, where cartoon movies like *Cinderella*, *Snow White*, and *Fantasia* were drawn. It has now become one of the biggest Hollywood studios and the owner of eleven theme parks around the world. The company now produces videos (*Cinderella II* and *III*) and live-action films (*The Princess Diaries*), owns cable and television networks (the Disney Channel, ESPN, and ABC), and has cruise ships. It also sells toys, clothing, and other consumer products.

Based on the success of Disney World and Disneyland, the Walt Disney Company decided to explore the idea of building theme parks in countries outside of the United States. It first established theme parks in Tokyo in 1983. The Euro Disney Resort was built outside Paris, France, in 1992. Hong Kong Disney was built in 2005. When the company first decided to build these theme parks, much consideration had to be given to each country's culture and how to best respect it while introducing the population to the very American Disney phenomenon. For example, Disney representatives sampled lots of local foods to decide what to offer at the theme parks' restaurants and concession stands. They tried to steep themselves in local

Disney Works Its Magic

The Hong Kong Disneyland, which opened in 2005, created new jobs for local residents. The park's designers took into consideration the cultural differences in Hong Kong. They paid special attention to things that would make its Chinese visitors feel welcome. The designers were careful to include the principles of feng shui, which is the Chinese art of placing objects in harmony with their environment. They made sure to offer Chinese cuisine, and they built a garden filled with statues of Disney characters to satisfy the Chinese interest in tourist photography. To communicate with guests, the park's employees speak both English and Chinese, including the Cantonese and Mandarin dialects of China. Guide maps are printed in a number of languages in order to accommodate the park's diverse international guests.

Walt Disney Company decided to try its hand at parks around the world, such as this one in Paris, France. They make sure to feature the local culture and preferences in each park.

and national culture in order to make sure that the theme parks accurately reflected each country in a respectful and sensitive way.

When Disney was building the Euro Disney Resort in Paris, the company hired a panel of European consultants, including representatives from France, Switzerland, England, and Germany. Disney learned from this group that Europeans do not like to stand in line for their food. So, the company needed to adjust the way that it designed and operated the food courts and restaurants at the Euro Disney park. It also decided to have more restaurants and fewer snack food options because Europeans do not eat as much as Americans do. They instead linger over meals longer than most American diners. Europeans also prefer to eat outside when the weather is nice. So, when Disney was designing eating areas, it planned for more than 2,100 outdoor seats.

CHAPTER 5

On the Move: The Role of Immigration

G lobalization has long provided a means for people to move from country to country. When a company relocates its headquarters, for example, and offers workers the chance of moving too, employees must decide what's best for their families. Other times, the economic conditions of a nation may provide little or no opportunities to make enough money to support a family. In those cases, workers seemingly have no choice but to move abroad, hoping for a better, more financially prosperous life. Meanwhile, in other instances, the horrors of constant war compel people to flee their native lands. In each case, immigration may seem the only viable option, compelling people to relocate to a strange land of opportunity.

According to the World Bank, the number of people living outside their country of origin grew during the 1990s, rising from 120 million in 1990 to about 200 million in 2008. Many are leaving their countries of origin to seek a better life and more opportunities elsewhere. Some are simply looking to improve their lot, while others leave home out of necessity. They can find

As people move to different areas of the world, they bring their
cultures with them. Although that is exciting and educational,
the clash of cultures can cause friction and stress.

no work where they live. If they hope to support their families and survive, they must leave their home countries and seek out employment elsewhere.

Just as businesses have become globalized, shifting operations to wherever the best opportunity is, so, too, have workers, who travel to where the jobs are. With the movement of people come the transfer of ideas, the introduction of new and different customs and cultures, and the threat of change to communities around the world. While this movement has been exciting, allowing people to learn about cultures around the world, it has also created stress and resistance. The movement of people and jobs has generated dislocations, friction, and anxiety all around the world.

Moving Across Borders

Globalization has led to the increased spread, or migration, of people around the world. By increasing the flow of information, improving communication, and making transportation faster and cheaper, globalization has also increased the number of jobs available in other countries. This causes people to migrate to those countries.

The migration of people across borders is not new. People have always left their homes in search of better opportunities, both within and outside of their own countries. Globalization has added a new dimension to this movement of workers, however. As businesses expand to include operations in foreign countries, globalization has made migration a necessity for many people. Their jobs at home may get sent overseas, where people are often willing to work for less money. This leaves the people who lost their jobs unemployed and without income (money coming in). There may be no jobs in their area anymore. So, they are forced to travel to where the jobs are—in another town, county, state, or even country.

Immigrant Culture in the United States

More and more people who were born outside the United States are traveling to America to live and work. These people are changing America even as they adopt its ways. More than a million immigrants arrive in the United States each year, most of them from Latin America or Asia. Since

The number of Latin American people moving to the
United States to live and work since 1990 has exploded.

1990, the number of foreign-born US residents has risen by six million to just more than twenty-five million. This is the biggest immigration wave since the turn of the twentieth century. English may be one of the world's most spoken languages, but in some parts of the United States, it is now second to Spanish. The US population is expected to grow by fifty million in the next twenty-five years. Half of that increase will probably be due to immigrants and the children of immigrants.

This renewed influx of foreigners into the United States has sparked outrage and fear among some Americans. Some people fear losing their jobs to an immigrant who might be willing to work for less. Others are not comfortable with the customs or culture of newly arrived residents. Many Americans argue that borders should be closed to all new immigration or that only people from certain countries should be allowed in the country. In some instances, immigrants have been harassed, attacked, and even killed.

The influx of foreigners in America has raised more than a few contentious questions about immigration.

What gets lost in the overheated passion of the immigration debate is the fact that all Americans (who are not Native Americans), no matter how many generations of their family have been in the country, are the descendants of immigrants. The ancestors of Americans entered the stream of globalization, most of them choosing to leave their homes for better economic, political, or personal opportunities in a new, rich, and abundant land. These early emissaries of globalization brought their cultural traditions with them and contributed to a new American culture that preached freedom, liberty, industry, and tolerance. Today's immigrants are merely adding new layers of richness to this New World culture.

Immigrants—the everyday foot soldiers of globalization who bravely forge ahead at its front lines—do not merely take the benefits and opportunities that working and living in the United States offer. For in return, they provide hard work, often in jobs that most Americans are unwilling to perform themselves. Their work and spending contribute to the local economy, even as they continue to support family members back in their home countries. They bring their cultural traditions and merge them with American culture, creating something new and stronger and richer. American culture is immigrant culture. And globalization is, and has always been, the spark of life that has created that culture and spread it across the world, allowing all to contribute to, borrow from, and share in the riches of other cultures. This is the shining promise of globalization, its most noble ideal, and its highest achievement.

Myths and Facts

Myth: Globalization is new.

Fact: Globalization may be moving at a much faster pace today, but it has been around for hundreds of years. For centuries, nations have bought from and sold to other countries and have established companies on foreign soil. This international exchange of goods and services is known as trade, and it is a major component of globalization.

Myth: Globalization is a force that will result in world peace.

Fact: Globalization leads to the spread of culture, languages, communication, ideas, and business. But it does not mean that people around the world are always ready and willing to welcome foreign influences. The mere exchange of money, jobs, goods, and services does not necessarily eliminate long-standing suspicions or grudges between nations. Sometimes, globalization can actually increase hard feelings or resentment when people feel their native culture is under assault by a foreign one or their jobs are being lost or exported to other countries.

Myth: Globalization only helps already rich nations get even richer, making poor nations poorer.

Fact: Globalization has helped developing countries expand into business areas where opportunities did not exist before. Through globalization, many nations become stronger and more economically diverse.

Graffiti line the walls of a dilapidated building in San Juan, Puerto Rico. A high poverty rate is among the many hardships contributing to the island nation's financial struggles.

CHAPTER 6
Globalization Today

As we've discovered, globalization has an impact on financial systems, technology, health, culture, immigration, the development of poor nations, the environment, and the production of energy to power our homes and businesses. Today, three areas that have sparked much attention are financial systems, health, and immigration.

During the US recession from December 2007 to June 2009, the country's financial troubles had a negative impact on global markets. More recently, Puerto Rico, Greece, and China each encountered devastating financial crises in 2015. As of summer 2015, Puerto Rico owed more than $70 billion in debt. Attributing to the staggering amount of debt were a decline in tourism, high unemployment, high poverty, and other issues. As a result, its governor sought to file bankruptcy. The challenge is that because of its island structure, Puerto Rico was not able to take advantage of that legal remedy. The result has been increased financial strain and continued debt issues. By all accounts, investors worried that Puerto Rico would default on its loans, representing the largest default in this country.

In a global economy, what happens in one country impacts another. As the United States grappled with its economic crises in 2007–2009, other

Puerto Rico's Governor Alejandro Garcia Padilla (center). Puerto Rico, along with China and Greece, has struggled to deal with financial crisis in 2015. It owed more than $70 billion.

countries experienced similar financial troubles. Unexpectedly in 2009, according to a recent *New York Times* article, Greece announced it had been understating certain financial figures for years. That triggered fears that Greece was not as financially sound as investors believed. Soon Greece could not borrow, resulting in near bankruptcy by 2010. Two financial bailouts helped Greece, yet its debt issues continued. At the height of its financial problems, the country took severe measures—including temporarily closing banks—to limit its citizens' cash after a run on banks as Greek citizens withdrew money at alarming rates. Greece received emergency bailout assistance in summer 2015. Greece's situation did not impact other global markets as severely as some expected.

As the 2007–2008 financial crises in the United States ricocheted through-out the world, China was also affected. For example, China introduced a stimulus package in 2008 to help spark its economic strength after Leh-man Brothers collapsed in the United States. One of the outcomes was increased debt that some analysts believe led to an unstable Chinese stock market. At first, the stock market expanded, including a surge from mid-2014 to mid-2015. That changed after the stock market hit a record high on June 12, 2015, followed by sharp declines in subsequent days. Although the government attempted to halt the decline, China's stock market woes continued plaguing the country. At first, it appeared as if China's situation would not have a significant impact. That changed on August 24 when the

As China's stock market plummeted sharply in the summer of 2015, worried traders in the United States could only watch as US and other stock markets seemed to follow suit.

stock market crashed in China. China's "Black Monday" impacted US and other markets, resulting in significant stock value losses for other countries, including investors in the United States. The government implemented measures to bolster its stock market. However, the crisis continues to spark investor fears through the early part of the fourth quarter of 2015.

The United States Tackles Immigration

Because of its proximity to Mexico, for example, Arizona has been particularly concerned about Mexican citizens fleeing the drug-torn country and entering into Arizona. In 2010, based on this concern, Arizona passed a law to bar illegal immigration. It, among other things, requires police to question the status of people suspected of being illegal immigrants. It does not require that illegal immigrants be deported, but the state can choose to do so. The law has been challenged in various courts, with some of its provisions struck down. However, the Supreme Court has upheld much of the law, including the requirement mentioned earlier.

Following Arizona's example, Alabama, Georgia, Indiana, and other states passed laws restricting immigration. Moreover, other states have adopted other laws that limit immigration or immigrants' rights. Texas, for example, was sued in July 2015 for withholding birth certificates from children born in the United States to illegal immigrants. That case was still pending.

On the national level, President Barack Obama in 2012 introduced a "deferred action" program benefiting undocumented students. It enabled them to go to school and get jobs without fear of being deported. In November 2014, he announced further immigration policy measures. Significantly, the policy offers a "deal" to illegal immigrants to stay in the United States without fear of deportation if they meet specific criteria. It is specifically designed to help non-criminals. In announcing the policy, President Obama noted: ". . .we're going to keep focusing enforcement resources on actual threats to our security. Felons, not families. Criminals, not children. Gang members, not a mom who's working hard to provide for her kids. We'll prioritize, just like law enforcement does every day." Implementation of the policy has been blocked due to court rulings.

Abroad, immigration has also proved a similarly thorny globalization concern.

Fleeing Immigrants

Desperation has fueled efforts by individuals throughout the world to flee from war especially. According to the United Nations, "there are currently some 43 million uprooted victims of conflict and persecution worldwide. More than 15 million of them are refugees who have fled their countries, while another 27 million are people who remain displaced by conflict inside their own homelands—so-called 'internally displaced people.'" According to the United Nations, the UN High Commissioner for Refugees (UNHCR), for example, ". . .helps some 4.8 million registered Palestine refugees in Jordan, Lebanon, Syria and the occupied Palestinian territory."

Sadly, illegal crossings into other countries have resulted in catastrophic results. Numerous incidents have been reported of refugees drowning after small boats have capsized in the Mediterranean Sea. These include heartbreaking incidents that occurred in Greece and Libya. In other cases, as was in Austria, overstuffed vehicles result in most —if not all—individuals dying of suffocation.

Unfortunately, while refugees are fleeing, some of those safe countries are closing their doors. In September 2015, Denmark closed its border with

Immigration has become a controversial globalization issue. Some
feel they have no other choice but to flee their country and seek
refuge elsewhere, such as this Syrian refugee in 2015.

Germany after safety concerns sparked by people's use of a high-speed motor-
way to enter the country. That month, Germany instituted temporary border
controls for security reasons. Shortly after, Poland, Hungary, Austria, and Denmark all announced plans to control their borders, limiting immigrant access.
Hungary warned it would deport individuals illegally entering the country.

What has caused the shift in perception and moved countries to ban
rather than welcome immigrants? While some countries acknowledge that
people fleeing war-torn countries need a place of a sanctuary and safety,
many are not willing to absorb the costs of housing unemployed citizens
of another nation. Similarly, language barriers and need for necessities such
as food and shelter have caused some countries to block immigrants. There

has been some recent developments in this area. Prior to the border control measure, Germany had committed to keep its borders open to significantly more refugees and pledged billions in financial help—but it also indicated other European countries should also assist in the effort.

Continuing Trend

Globalization spurs peoples' movement from one country to another. Thanks to technological advances, people can more easily determine which country may provide a safe haven where financial opportunities exist. Perhaps in these places jobs are plentiful and housing is affordable. As such, the influx of immigrants to various countries is not likely to be hindered by the examples of the countries mentioned above—Germany, Poland, Hungary, Austria, and Denmark. Rather, people will continue to try legal—and illegal methods—of entering another location. Whether restrictive border controls will remain is unclear. What is clear is that immigration will continue to be a globalization issue countries will grapple with in the near future.

How Can You Help?

As a student there are things you can do to get involved:

- **Be informed.** Know what the debate is and know how you feel about it. Get information that will help you articulate your position.

- **Be transparent.** Have members of your family recently immigrated to this country? If so, share with friends and others the journey to America and why this nation was chosen as an ideal place to settle.

Students can help bring attention to a global issue with a demonstration or a dance, like these students in a One Billion Rising event highlighting domestic abuse victims.

- **Provide cultural awareness.** Your cultural identity is important. Be open to sharing information about your culture—be it language, food, or traditions to help others become more knowledgeable and comfortable.

- **Reach out.** If you've ever moved to a new area, you know how difficult that can be. Reach out to new students in your school who have recently moved to the United States. It's not necessary to be excessively extraverted, or outgoing. Just try to be friendly. Make yourself available to assist and open to new friendships, if the opportunity arises.

- **Report bullying.** Sometimes, cultural sensitivity results in bullying. If you notice other students bullying immigrants, report it. Be brave enough to stand up for those who may be afraid to stand up for themselves.

The Bottom Line

Many people fight immigration because they believe non-citizens take jobs and use resources that should be available to them. This is true, in some respect. However, is blocking all immigrants the answer? Each country must decide for itself. In the United States, however, it is important to remember our immigrant history and continue to welcome others so that

Globalization is a touchy immigration issue, but keep in mind
that the United States was founded by immigrants with hopes
that it would become a country of opportunity for all.

our nation will always be a refuge and land of opportunity—for citizens and immigrants alike.

Globalization refers to the increased international movement of people, knowledge, ideas, products, and money. Immigration addresses just one of the people issues affecting globalization. Globalization's influence on so many facets of our everyday lives is an ever-evolving trend that is fascinating to watch unfold. As we shop, eat, connect (in person and online) with people from all over the world, and use global products we come to realize the numerous advantages of globalization. Indeed, today, we enjoy many global benefits not available at any other time in the world's history. What a privilege and responsibility!

Globalization Timeline

1800s East India Company brought cotton, silk, dye, and tea to America's shores for sale.

1892 Coca-Cola founded.

1929–1930s 1929 Stock Market Crash in United States affects world.

1944 World Bank established with headquarters in Washington, D.C. with mission of "ending and boosting" shared prosperity.

May 1945 End of World War II.

1945–1991 The Cold War era of tension between United States and Soviet Union.

October 24, 1945 United Nations established.

December 27, 1945 International Monetary Fund established to "foster global monetary cooperation" and other initiatives.

1962 Wal-Mart founded.

1967 First international locations of McDonald's open in Canada and Puerto Rico.

1971 Starbucks founded.

June 1972 The United Nations Environment Programme created

1973 Oil crises impacts nations.

1981 First personal computer introduced by IBM, paving way for technological advances that would in future advance globalization.

October 1987 Stock market crash reveals impact of economic globalization.

December 1991 Soviet Union dissolves.

1993 European Union established.

1994 Interest in Internet begins switching to non-technical, non-academic use.

January 1, 1995 World Trade Organization established in Geneva, Switzerland.

2000s–Present Outsourcing of jobs overseas results in lost jobs in United States

February 2004 Facebook launched, connecting people all over the globe.

March 2006 Twitter established.

December 2007 Great Recession begins; impacts other countries.

2014 Ebola epidemic hits West Africa; impacts other nations.

Bibliographic Sources

Andreeva, Nellie. "'NCIS' 'Modern Family' Most Watched Series In The World & Other Monte-Carlo TV Awards." Deadline, June 11, 2014. Retrieved August 11, 2015 (http://deadline.com/2014/06/ncis-modern-family-most-watched-series-in-the-world-monte-carlo-tv-festival-awards-787408/).

Areddy, James T. "China Stock Market Woes Have Roots in 2008 Stimulus." *The Wall Street Journal,* July 10, 2015.

Balko, Radley. "A Valentine to Globalization." Fox News. February 13, 2003. Retrieved October 1, 2008 (http://www.foxnews.com/story/0,2933,78416,00.html).

Bhagwati, Jagdish. *In Defense of Globalization.* New York, NY: Oxford University Press, 2007.

Bouras, Stelios and Nektaria Stamouli. "Greeks Yanks Bank Deposits as Talks Falter." *The Wall Street Journal,* June 20, 2015.

Buzzle.com. "Pros and Cons of Globalization." Retrieved September 18, 2008 (http://www.buzzle.com/articles/pros-and-cons-of-globalization.html).

CBS News. "Where's the Beef? Meatless McDonald's Burgers in India."
    April 2, 2007. Retrieved October 26, 2008 (http://www.cbsnews.
    com/stories/2007/04/02/asia_letter/main2640540.shtml).

Eitzen, D. Stanley, and Maxine Baca Zinn. *Globalization: The
    Transformation of Social Worlds.* Boston, MA: Wadsworth, 2008.

Friedman, Thomas L. *The Lexus and the Olive Tree: Understanding
    Globalization.* Norwell, MA: Anchor Press, 2000.

Globalist. "Coke—Globalization's Real Thing." April 4, 2001. Retrieved
    September 20, 2008 (http://www.theglobalist.com/DBWeb/StoryId
    .aspx?StoryId=2004).

Hayes, Jack. "Disney Magic Spreads Across the Atlantic; Popular U.S.
    Theme Park Prepares for Opening of Euro Disney Resort Near Paris
    in April '92." BNET Business Network. October 28, 1991. Retrieved
    October 22, 2008 (http://findarticles.com/p/articles/mi_m3190/is_
    n42_v25/ai_11426102).

Ignatius, David. "A Global Marketplace Means Global Vulnerability."
    GlobalPolicy.org. June 22, 1999. Retrieved September 18, 2008
    (http://www.globalpolicy.org/globaliz/special/globvuln.htm).

Ip, Greg, and Jon Hilsenrath. "Crises Fall Short of Going Global."
    The Wall Street Journal, July 11, 2015.

Kimball, Will and Robert E. Scott. "China Trade, Outsourcing and
    Jobs. Growing U.S. Trade Deficit with China Cost 3.2 Million Jobs
    Between 2001 and 2013, with Job Losses in Every State." Economic
    Policy Institute. December 11, 2014. Retrieved August 11, 2015
    (http://www.epi.org/publication/china-trade-outsourcing-and-jobs/).

Knight, Deborah. "Globalization: Take Advantage of a Shrinking World." SFGate.com. August 14, 2005. Retrieved September 18, 2008 (http://www.sfgate.com/cgi-bin/article.cgi?f=/g/a/2005/08/14/padams.DTL).

Krogstad, Jens Manuel, and Jeffrey S. Passel. "5 Facts About Illegal Immigration in the U.S." Pew Research Center. July 4, 2015. Retrieved September 12, 2015 (http://www.pewresearch.org/fact-tank/2015/07/24/5-facts-about-illegal-immigration-in-the-u-s/).

LeGrain, Philippe. "Cultural Globalization Is Not Americanization." Chronicle of Higher Education. May 9, 2003. Retrieved September 20, 2008 (http://chronicle.com/free/v49/i35/35b00701.htm).

Longworth, Richard C. *Caught in the Middle: America's Heartland in the Age of Globalism.* New York, NY: Bloomsbury USA, 2007.

Marling, William H. *How "American" Is Globalization?* Baltimore, MD: Johns Hopkins University Press, 2006.

Overholt, William H. "Globalization's Unequal Discontents." Washington Post. December 21, 2006. Retrieved October 22, 2008 (http://www.washingtonpost.com/wp-dyn/content/article/2006/12/20/AR2006122001307.html).

McHugh, Jess. "China's 'Black Monday' Timeline: The Chinese Stock Market and How it Happened." *International Business Times.* August 24, 2015. Retrieved September 12, 2015 (http://www.ibtimes.com/china-black-monday-timeline-chinese-stock-market-crash-how-it-happened-2065173).

People's Daily. "Disneyland to Bring Opportunities, Challenges to HK Tourism." February 21, 2001. Retrieved October 22, 2008 (http://english.peopledaily.com.cn/200102/21/eng20010221_62961.html).

Riggs, Fred W. "Globalization: Key Concepts." July 29, 2000. Retrieved October 22, 2008 (http://www2.hawaii.edu/~fredr/glocon.htm#CHASE1).

Steinhauser, Gabriele. "Can Greece Default on Debt but Keep Euro?" *The Wall Street Journal,* June 16, 2015.

Steinhauser, Gabriele, Viktoria Dendrinou, and Matthew Dalton. "Eurozone Leaders Reach Rescue Deal for Greece, With Tough Conditions." *The Wall Street Journal,* July 13, 2015.

Stiglitz, Joseph E. *Globalization and Its Discontents.* New York, NY: W. W. Norton & Co., 2003.

The *New York Times* "Greece Debt Crises Explained." August 20, 2015. Retrieved September 12, 2015 (http://www.nytimes.com/interactive/2015/business/international/greece-debt-crisis-euro.html?_r=0).

The White House. Transcript of "Remarks by the President in Address to the Nation on Immigration." November 20, 2014. Retrieved September 13, 2015 (https://www.whitehouse.gov/issues/immigration/immigration-action#).

United Nations. "Refugees: Overview of Forced Displacement." Retrieved September 11, 2015 (http://www.un.org/en/globalissues/briefingpapers/refugees/overviewofforceddisplacement.html).

White, Andrew. "From the Living Room to the World: The Globalization of Television News." Retrieved October 1, 2008 (http://homepage.newschool.edu/~chakravs/andrew.html).

White, Gillian B. "What's Really Happening in Puerto Rico?" *The Atlantic.* June 29, 2015. Retrieved August 11, 2015 (http://www .theatlantic.com/business/archive/2015/06/puerto-rico-debt-crisis/ 397241/)

World Bank. "Topics/Policy/Overview." Updated April 6, 2015. Retrieved August 13, 2015 (http://www.worldbank.org/en/topic/ poverty/overview).

Glossary

bhangra—A popular dance music originating chiefly in the south Asian immigrant community of England. It combines traditional Punjabi music with elements of disco and hip-hop.

biofuel—A fuel composed of, or produced from, biological raw materials. Examples are wood or ethanol.

capital—Another word for money or wealth, especially when used for investments and to build businesses.

consumer—A person who buys or uses a product or service.

dialect—A regional version of a language that is distinguished by different vocabulary, grammar, and pronunciation from other regional varieties of the same language.

ethanol—A colorless liquid used as an additive to fuel.

export—To send products to another country.

feng shui—A Chinese practice combining spirituality and design in which a structure or site is chosen or configured so as to be in harmony with its environment, thereby promoting smooth functioning, good fortune, and positive outcomes.

fuel cell—A device that continuously changes the chemical energy of a fuel (such as hydrogen) and an oxidant directly into electrical energy.

globalism—A national policy of treating the whole world as a sphere for political and economic influence.

goods—Products that are made and sold to consumers.

import—To bring products into a country.

migration—The movement of people from one country, place, or locality to another.

vegetarian—Describes a dietary practice that includes the avoidance of meat and animal-derived foods and products.

Westernization—The social process of becoming familiar with or converting to the customs and practices of Western civilization.

Further Reading

Books

Catel, Patrick. *Money and Trade.* Chicago, IL: Heinemann Library, 2012.

Chander, Anupam. *The Electronic Silk Road: How the Web Binds the World in Commerce.* New Haven, CT: Yale University Press, 2013.

Fay, Gail. *Economies Around the World.* Chicago: Heinemann Library, 2012.

Hicks, Terry Allan. *The Pros and Cons of Oil.* New York, NY: Cavendish Square Publishing, 2015.

Johnson, Robin (Robin R.) *The Economics of Making a Movie.* New York, NY: Crabtree Publishing Company, 2014.

McManus, Lori. *Money through History.* Chicago, IL: Heinemann Library, 2012.

Spilsbury, Richard. *Global Economy.* Chicago, IL: Heinemann Library, 2012.

Steger, Manfred B. *Globalization: A Very Short Introduction.* Third Ed. New York, NY: Oxford University Press, 2013.

Sylvester, Kevin and Michael Hlinka. *Follow Your Money: Who Gets It, Who Spends It, Where Does It Go?* New York, NY: Annick Press, 2013.

Websites

Global Policy Forum
www.globalpolicy.org/about-gpf-mm.html
This organization's website offers reports, a newsletter, and other information on global issues.

Globalization 101
www.globalization101.org/
This website includes resources and tools for students on various globalization topics.

Teaching with the World Peace Game
www.worldpeacegame.org/2-uncategorised/32-john-hunters-tedtalk
This video of the "World Peace Game" features the inventor discussing a game that teaches globalization and its global impact.

The Economics of Globalization
unausa.org/global-classrooms-model-un/for-educators/curriculum/
economics-of-globalization
This website features student magazines on globalization, trade, and other topics from the United Nations Association of the United States of America.

Youth Flash Newsletter
undesadspd.org/Youth/YouthFlashNewsletter.aspx
This publication of United Nations Environment Programme is designed to provide youth with information on globalization issues.

World Bank

www.worldbank.org/en/about

The World Bank strives to reach two goals by 2030: "The World Bank Group has set two goals for the world to achieve by 2030: 'End extreme poverty by decreasing the percentage of people living on less than $1.25 a day to no more than 3%' and 'Promote shared prosperity by fostering the income growth of the bottom 40% for every country.'

Index